The Magic of Music

12 Imaginative Solos for Late Elementary Pianists

Dennis Alexander

Foreword

I've always felt that music inspires magic. Everyone who experiences the joy of making some kind of music develops the ability to discover this magic in one way or another. Perhaps it is that special feeling which occurs when a certain rhythm or colorful harmony touches the heart of the player. Or maybe it is that favorite melodic line which inspires one to "sing inside" and feel the warmth of a beautifully turned phrase. The pieces in this collection are designed to entertain, reinforce and enhance the important musical and technical skills which are being developed at the late elementary level. Whether it is the swaying palm trees in "Laguna Breezes," the robust rhythms of "Right Uptown!" or the gentle, flowing new age patterns of "Windsong," students will develop their own magical imagination through the repertoire that is contained in this collection! I wish you much success and enjoyment as you journey through "The Magic of Music."

Dennis Alexander

Contents

for Matthew Moisen

Right Uptown!

Dennis Alexander

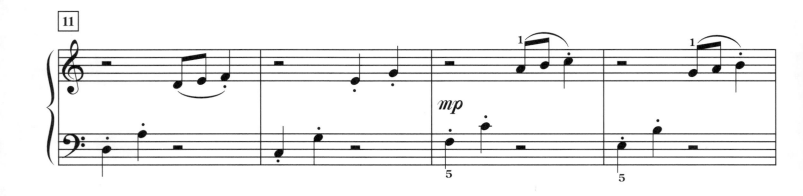

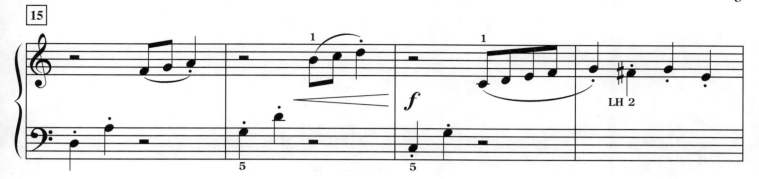

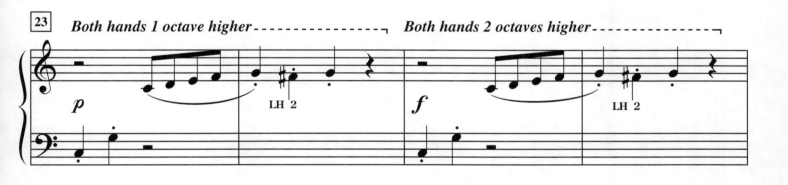

Cozy Thoughts

Dennis Alexander

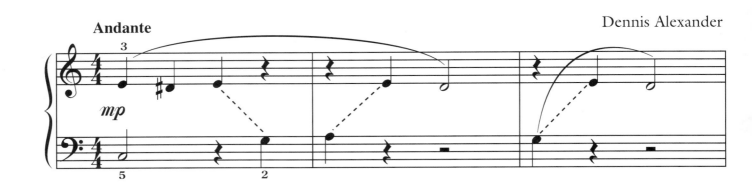

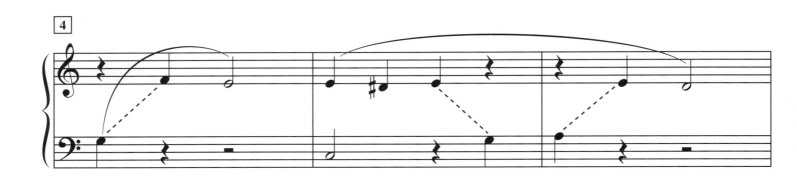

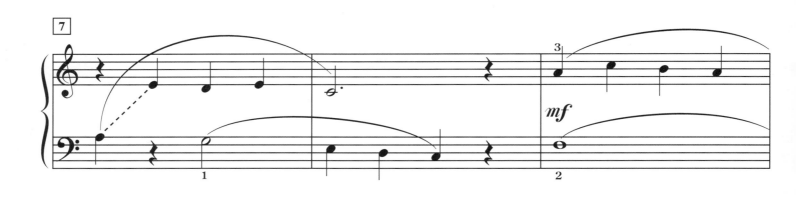

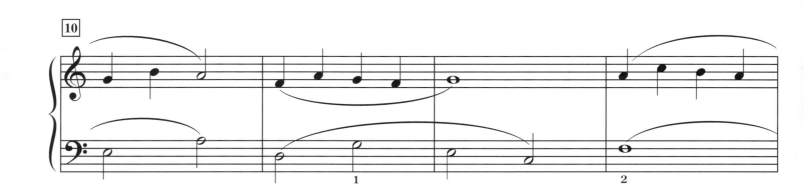

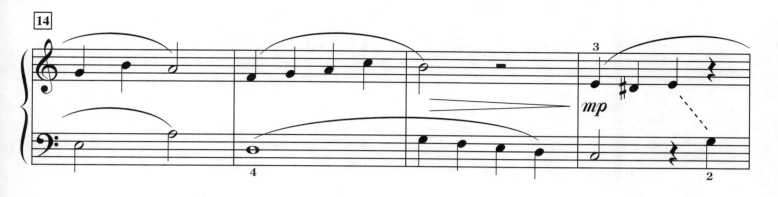

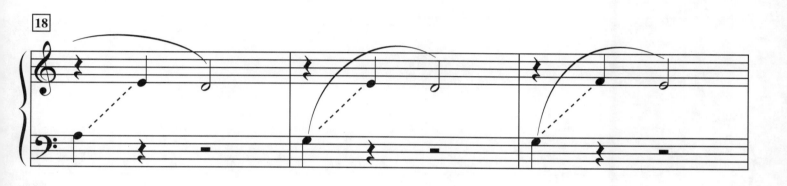

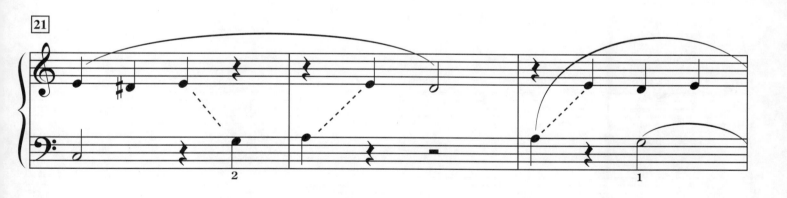

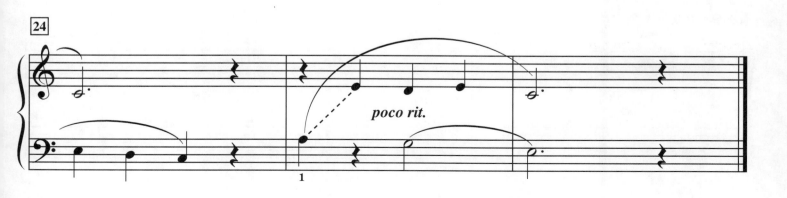

Sharp Ahoy

Dennis Alexander

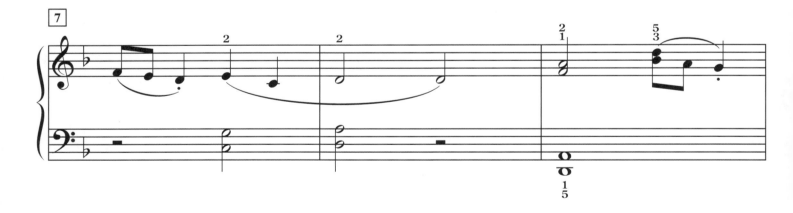

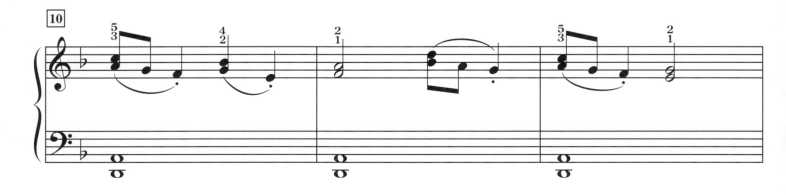

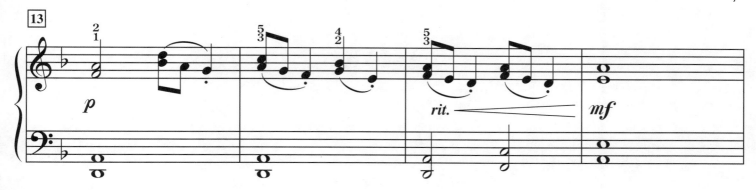

A-OK

Dennis Alexander

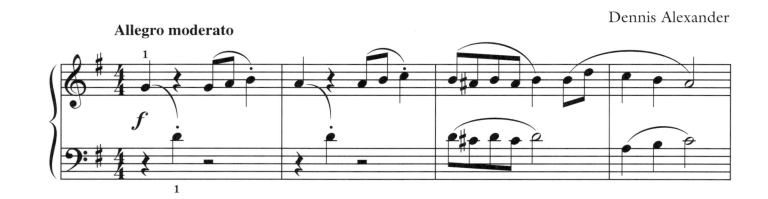

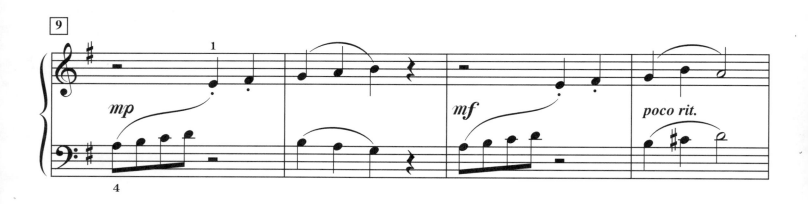

Mountain Dance

Dennis Alexander

for Ramin Azhir

Bells of San Miguel

Dennis Alexander

Mixed-Up Martians

Dennis Alexander

Allegro moderato

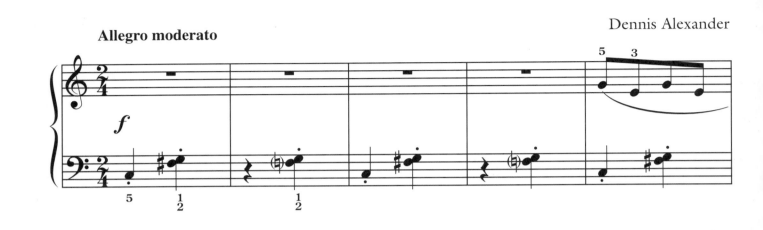

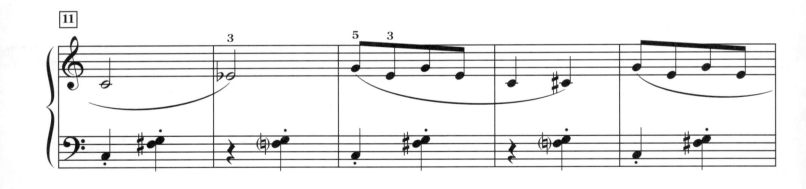

to Coda ⊕

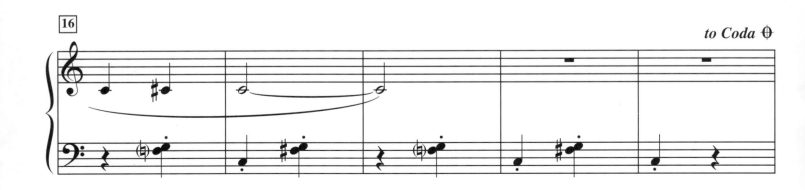

21

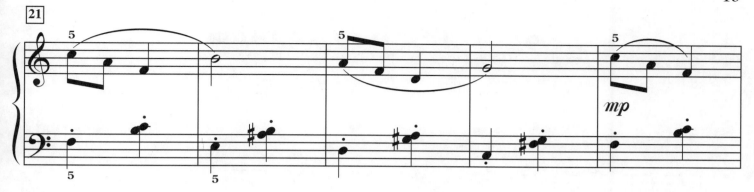

26

D. C. al Coda

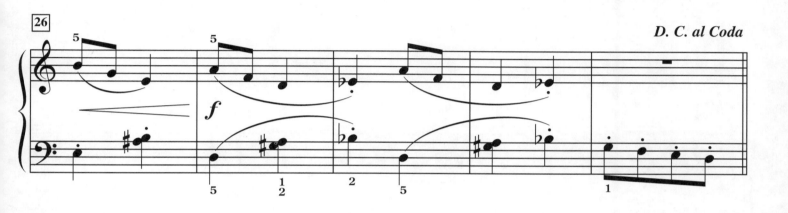

Ⓕ *Coda*

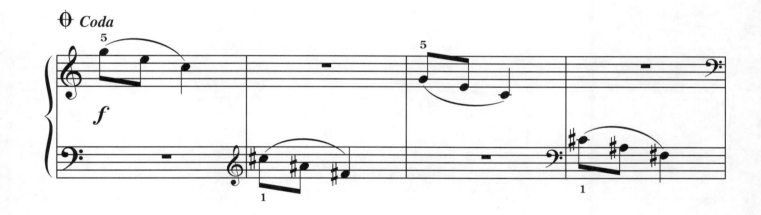

35

Got Those Boogie Blues

Dennis Alexander

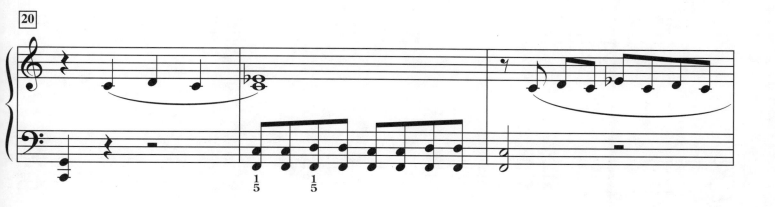

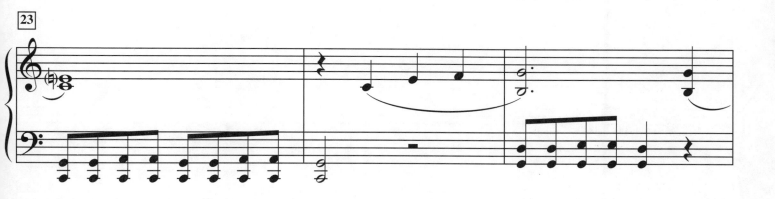

D. C. al Fine

Danse Brusque

Dennis Alexander

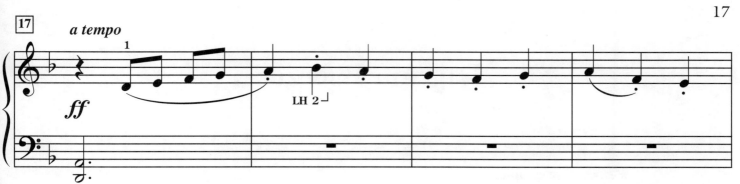

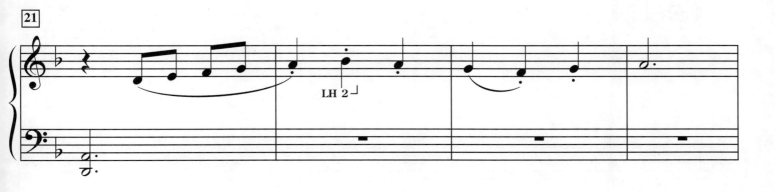

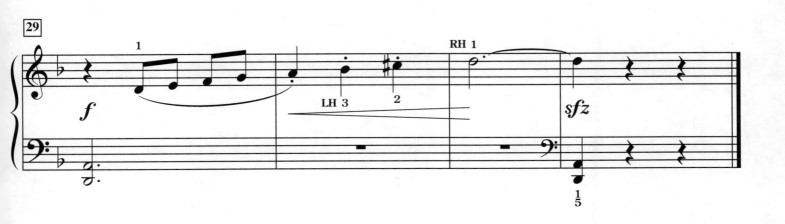

for Chandler Moisen

Laguna Breezes

Dennis Alexander

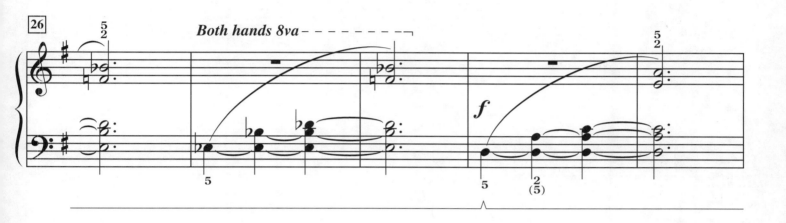

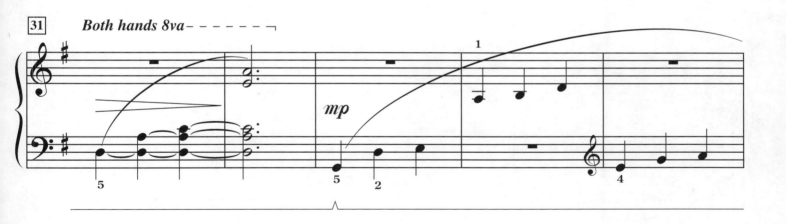

Sometimes ★

Teneramente

Dennis Alexander

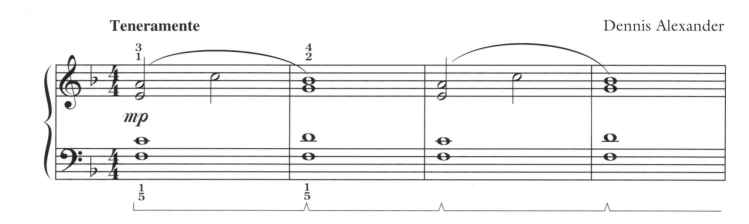

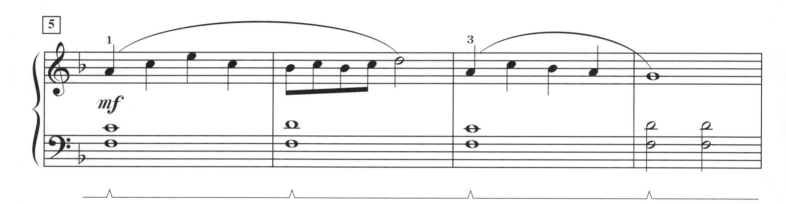

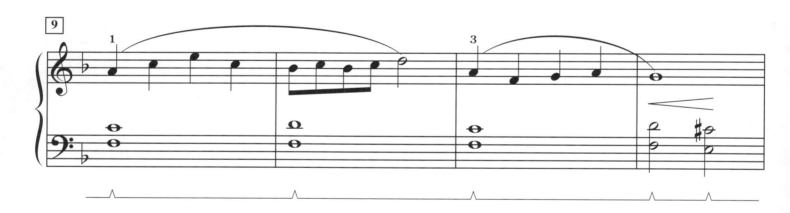

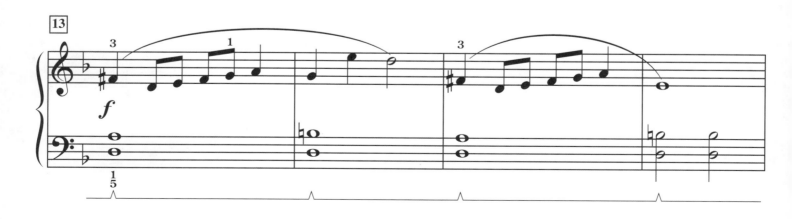

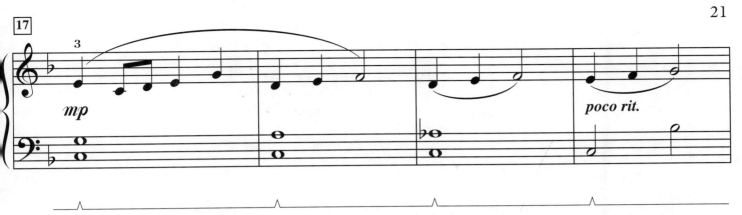

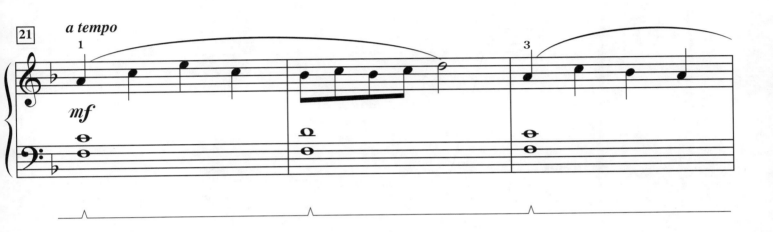

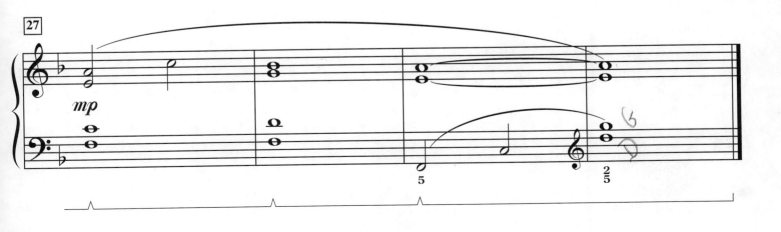

★Windsong

Dennis Alexander

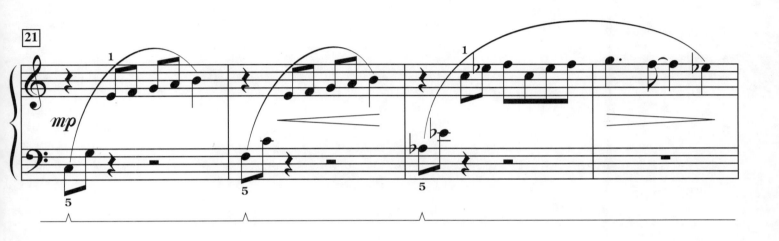

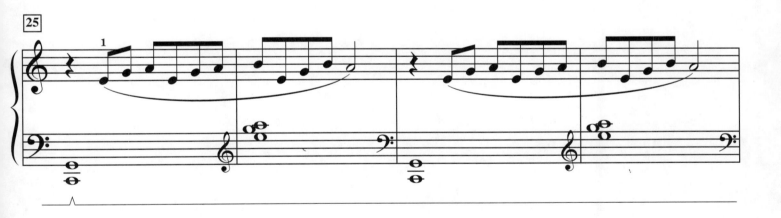